The pilgrimage

And if I speak of belonging,
then I speak of bodies prostrating
of women holding onto the backs of their husbands as they
are guided through herds of people dressed in white.

And if I speak of belonging,
I speak of others at home,
kneeling on scented prayer mats,
joining their brothers who plead on
the heated plains of *Arafah*.

And if I speak of belonging,
I speak of those who supplicate
to be pilgrims next year,
who circle the house of God,
begging to be forgiven.

And if I speak of belonging,
I speak of the barren mother
who cleanses in holy *zam zam,*
and whispers to her stomach,
anticipating life.

And if I speak of belonging,
I speak of those breathing their last,
wishing they had visited the Kabah
to revel in its beauty,
before returning to Him.

chai

cannot be made

in a kettle

chai

cannot be made

in a kettle

Juwairiah

First published 2023 by Lote Tree Press

www.lotetreepress.com

Hardback ISBN: 978-1-7394601-1-2

Paperback ISBN: 978-1-7394601-0-5

Also available as an ebook

Designed by Maktaba

www.maktaba.co.uk

A CIP catalogue record for this book is available from the British Library *for all those who have poured into my cup*

- (you know who you are).

CONTENTS

poems of diaspora and belonging

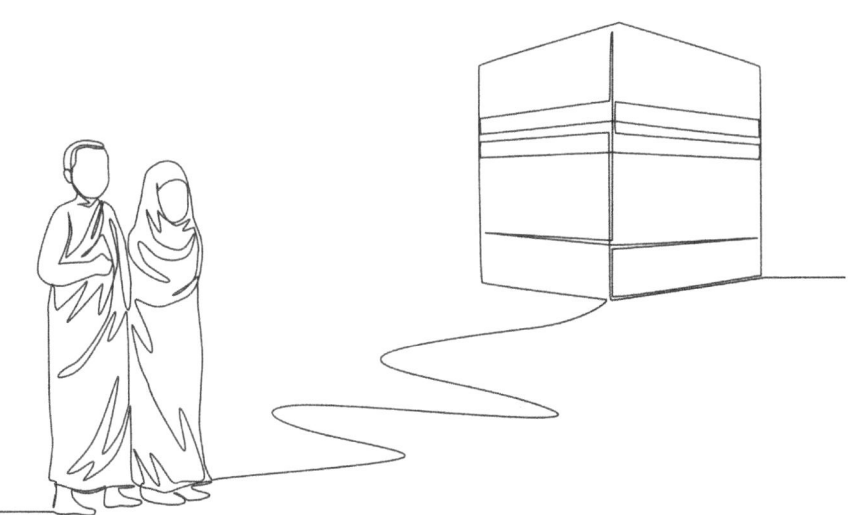

chai cannot be made in a kettle

The house

with two roofs

My daughter,
was conceived on neutral territory,
somewhere between Kenya and India.
She holds the keys to different dialects securely in her
mouth.

Some mornings,
I peep through the keyhole,
watch her and her father converse in Swahili.
I do not understand their language so instead,
I watch her tongue dance.
In those moments,
she is **his** pillar.

Some nights,
mid nightmare,
she calls for me in Gujarati.
I cradle her and sing an Indian lullaby.
In those moments,
she is **my** window.

But most days,
she moves boldly from room to room,
dipping in different languages,
refusing to pick one.
On those days,
she is our entire house.

chai cannot be made in a kettle

Yearning for our Beloved

I yearn to write about him, our Beloved. Some nights, I spill ink
onto paper, write and rewrite sentences – trembling violently,
as he did in Cave Hira.

I yearn to write about him, our Beloved. Find me hunched,
digging for words weighty enough - to treasure the tears
that his soaked beard carried, when he cried out - *ya ummati.*

I yearn to write about him, our Beloved. To understand how
such beauty sat, with blood-soaked sandals at Taif - merciful
enough to decline the Angel's offer.

I yearn to write about him, our Beloved. Let me linger in places
where his faithful companions gathered. Pocket the blessings,
of his presence.

I yearn to write about our Beloved. To stride on the streets,
where he conveyed the message of his Lord, to prostate my
body rhythmically in congregation.

I yearn to write about him, our Beloved, but I am unable to contain his greatness - within a line, a stanza, a poem.

I yearn to write about our Beloved – but instead I shall follow in his footsteps.

poems of diaspora and belonging

In and out

We surrendered syllables so that we would fit in,
muted rhymes and rhythms so we weren't booted out.

Practiced proper pronunciation to dig in
to the leftover morsels of our culture we threw out.

Feasted on the flesh of our forefathers to cave in
to mass murder of our mother tongue that is hung out.

Confine us back to our cells so we can be filled in,
like a diversity tick box to help you check out.

Yes, we are accustomed to this behaviour,
of being in and out.

The Open Mosque

From *Fajr* until *Isha,* the mosque remains open.
Calling the heartbroken and happy, for everyone it is open.

The *Imam* calls the *Adhaan* melodiously in ancient Arabic,
paving a pathway for believers, like a closed door, now open.

On Summer evenings, the pitter patter of the young,
rush towards the mosque, waiting eagerly to watch the dome open.

An elderly worshipper remains in *sujood* for half of the night,
knowing he will meet his Creator, praying his *Jannah* remains open.

A young woman fiddles with her hijab, nervous to enter the mosque.
A revert to Islam, she mumbles a silent prayer, for her heart to stay open.

It is very different now, believers pray at home.
 Juwairiah is amongst them.
They wait for the pandemic to pass,
so that the mosque can, once again, open.

No one uttered a word

The elderly sipped
offering the thieves
No one uttered a word
watched silently as they
into our brown,
No one uttered a word
The *chai* whirled in
swishing from
No one uttered a word
Temperatures rose,
they stole from us.
baptised them in English
named them
still no one

cold *desi chai*
the fresh pot.
when they stole from us,
poured their white
tainting our colours.
when they stole from us.
Dadda's saucepan,
side to side.
when they stole from us.
the *desi* spilled over,
Took our children
spring water
little Darjeelings,
uttered a word.

White Brownie

You aren't as unlucky as the others,
because you are a light skin brownie.

A not as dark as them brownie,
more of a milky brownie.

'I spent too long in the heat'
kinda brownie.

A brownie which doesn't scream
South Asian brownie.

The more acceptable,
Spanish brownie.

poems of diaspora and belonging

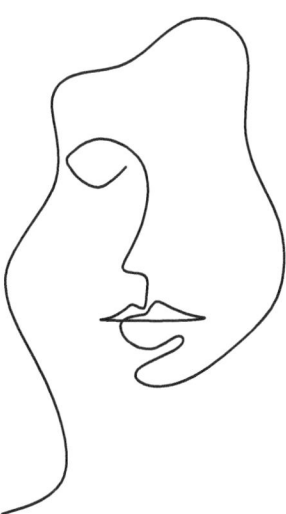

The Letterbox

i)

'Absolutely ridiculous that **they** choose to go around looking like letterboxes'.

ii)

Dear Boris,

The definition of a letter box is: *a box attached to an outside wall, or a slot in the door of a building, into which mail is delivered.* My mother, she dons a 'letterbox' every morning when she leaves the house. She does so, because she chooses to. Like a letterbox does, she swallows the letters whole. They disappear inside her and she protects them fiercely. She encapsulates their stories, and never discriminates against their stamp.

She receives letters from people in her community, strangers and friends alike. Unfortunately, sometimes even from people like you. Even then, she is unbiased,

26

non-judgmental and loving. She accepts them all willingly. She once received a letter from you.

When I suggested that she should get rid of your letter, she scolded me. She said, 'Everyone deserves a second chance," - that YOU too deserved to be loved.

Pure China

You swam out of my sister,

red and bloody,

with strawberry infused hair,

and dimples like craters,

embedded into the earth.

Dewy skin dipped in buttermilk,

and eyes as brown as baked clay.

I watched you greedily,

as though you were an

exhibition in a museum,

about to end.

You were like fine china

to be marveled at,

only from a distance,

to be brought out

when the special guests arrived.

I did not hold you for days,
your fragility and my tendency to break
precious things
a bad concoction.

Most nights
I watched your chest rise and fall,
rhythmically, in tune to a lullaby
only you knew.

On the seventh day
she named you,
Mariyah,
meaning pure.

On the eighth day,
I finally held you,
and whispered into your ear
that I would call you
Pure China.

chai cannot be made in a kettle

To remind myself
of your fragility,
and my tendency to break
precious things.

spring of '17

when we planted sunflowers in spring of '17
you held me tight and said
beginnings often hide themselves
in endings

you were diagnosed

I cradled myself into oblivion
stealing minutes of consciousness
between hospital stays and

burnt silence

now I'm at the end
searching for a new beginning
hoping that it's you.

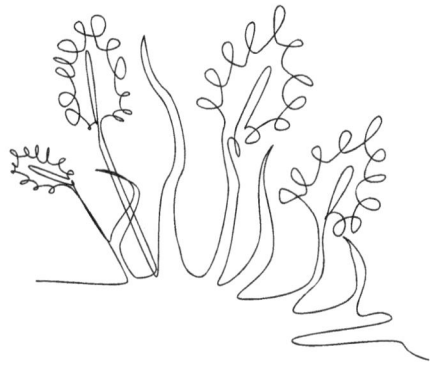

A prayer cycle

Fajr

Aubergine filled sky,
she weeps melodiously,
pleading with her God.

Dhuhr

During his lunch break,
he carves out fluent *Quran*,
forehead to the floor.

Asr

They dip their bodies.
In unity, they prostrate,
glorifying Him.

Magrib

She wraps her silk hair,

as the yolky sun blends red,

kneels to make *dua.*

Isha

Slumber tries to tug.

He lifts himself and stands tall,

in supplication.

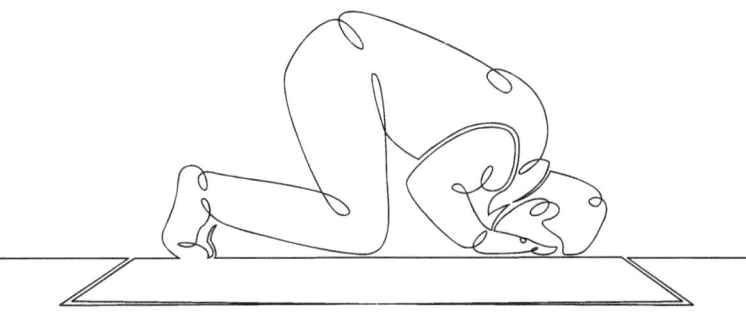

sacred women

I heard whispers of brown sacred women,
who lay under darkness, longing for their motherland.

A place where bodies bathe in sweet honey milk,
doused in ancient cardamom pods.

Where newborns suckle on cinnamon laced nipples,
under turmeric sun, satisfying themselves with Indian *lassi*.

I dig beneath layers of brown skin,
searching for the sacred woman within.

But there is no ache here,
instead only a motherless child.

poems of diaspora and belonging

For the next generation

We are not green fingered – but we try.

We plant seeds for our children –
for our children's children,
and for theirs after that.
Waiting for the flowers to blossom,
and fill the streets with colour.

We plant seeds for our babies –
our babies' babies and for theirs
after that. Hoping the flowers will
teach us how to have unconditional
colour for each other.

We pray loudly when planting,
we pray that the colour will help save
the red of our children.

Some of our flowers do not grow,
some are plucked far too early,
some are destroyed for being far too colourful.

Still we continue to plant flowers,
for our infants, our newborns,
and our fetuses. Praying that colour
will change the streets.

We are not green fingered – but we try.

we welcome submissions from underrepresented backgrounds

Please do tell us your stories,
you deserve to take up space.

Be raw, honest,
less open,
a little quieter,
be louder, just not here.
Please don't make a scene.

Red tape you see?
We can't publish that,
SPEAK for us; say we are
champions of diversity.

Diversify your work; branch out; maybe a little less
about blah-blah diversity, more about

love, young romance? Make sure you
include some identity poems; yes, some racism you
encountered.

It's too bland; talk more about how
you were targeted; more of your
working-class emotion.

Dig deeper, where did it hurt?
When they called you names..
Oh yes! perfect that time,

they pulled your hijab! Gosh that's terrible.
But do you have to wear that?

Eye-opening work: colonialism, chai, India.

We just don't want to alienate anyone,

you understand, right?

We need bame-working-class-poets. Thank you

for submitting your work; we regret to inform you

but there just isn't

enough

space.

No nicknames

Ignorant folk - before you ask me to shorten my name,
educate yourself on the importance of a noun.

The fragility of a name - like a museum it preserves
generations of the sacred - transports the blood of forefathers.

Pay respect to my skin - to the tongue of my
homeland – to the struggle of my grandfather
who carried pockets of Calcutta – the beat of its
street inscribed into his palms.

White birthed a genocide within the classroom – of
linguistics, words, letters, and rhythm.

We are here to reclaim – rebirth – to dip the tongues of
our young in shades of brown, inviting them back, unapologetic
with names with syllables - a few too many for you to
comprehend.

Chai cannot be made in a kettle

We sip *chai* as though it is holy / boil and brew water / infuse
cinnamon with fresh milk / dip spices into sacred saucepans and
dance / in colourful Saris to taunt the water to rise / howl silently
as it pours over edges / like a high tide spilling brown bodies.

Children gather sheepishly / with cupped hands / hoping to be
among the first /
to fill themselves with brown liquid / that holds the ingredients of
home.

Breathing on empty

My ancestors have not been granted the permission to heal
from the pain that has been rooted within them.
Their brown bodies lay lifeless, yearning to feel.

Their bones and limbs in denial, refuse to accept
that others watched silently as they suffered, unwilling to
condemn.
Their brown bodies lay lifeless, yearning to feel.

Their sanctified land now lays barren, unable to connect,
hunting desperately for compassion from a single stem.
Their brown bodies lay lifeless, yearning to feel.

During sacred nights, you hear the ghosts of those who wept,
and dug in parched earth, searching for the hidden gem.
My ancestors have not been granted the permission to heal.

The elderly remained alert, like hawks as the village slept,
collating the DNA from their mouths, through sacred phlegm.
Their brown bodies lay lifeless, yearning to feel.

The holy fragments of them that remains is kept

deep in the bosoms of their women.

My ancestors have not been granted the permission to heal.

Their brown bodies lay lifeless, yearning to feel.

chai cannot be made in a kettle

The black mamas who play

The kids in the playground grew tired
of the boy who always won.

He was never found when playing hide and seek,
nor caught when playing tag.

They didn't know the boy won
because his mama played with him religiously.

She taught him how to hold his breath,
how to be
nimble,
light,
small,
and
quiet.

How to be white,
so the hunters wouldn't find him.

And in between playing,

she taught him how to say please and thank you.

Just in case they did find him,

praying good manners would save him.

Something English

My mother swallowed it whole to keep it safe,
before swimming across blue to marry my father.

During labour, it swam out, flooding the walls
with orange, yellow and green.

They watched in admiration, both unaware,
that others were plotting to drown it.

They said it was damp, soaked in foreign tongue.
They offered a substitute, something dry,

But she absorbed it, refused to dilute it,
twirled with it in the Indian Ocean.

It ripples across waves, even to this day,

the name, Juwairiah

poems of diaspora and belonging

We are

The children of immigrants who speak broken English,
children of those who were broken by English,
children of those who the English broke,
children who are now broke because of the English,
immigrants of children who are mixed with English,
the English broke immigrants and their children.

Yes, we are,
those children,
and proud to be
Indian.

poems of diaspora and belonging

Indian British

(inspired by Raymond Antrobus – *Jamaican British*)

Many do not accept I am *Indian British*.
I speak English but with fragments of broken
Gujarati, no way could I be Indian British.

Skin too tanned to be one of us; skin too
fair to be one of them. Choose one,
Indian or British?

Stick the kettle on – tea – boil it in the
saucepan – *chai*. Which kind, Indian or British?

Indian only on a Friday night, spicy but not too spicy,
I can't take the heat - I'm British.

At school, laughed at the girl who spoke broken English.
At home, trying to mend my own mother tongue
neither - Indian nor British.

Someday coloniser – someday colonised.

Someday thief; someday victim. Who stole from who?

The Indian or the British?

chai cannot be made in a kettle

About the Author

Juwairiah is a poet and educator. Her first collection *chai cannot be made in a kettle* was birthed during the pandemic and written as part of her MA in Creative Writing and Education. The collection explores her identity as a British, Muslim, Indian woman living in London.

chai cannot be made in a kettle

Illustration acknowledgements

Vectortradition, Cover illustration
Aisha Nuraini, pages 11, 14, 27
Retany, page 12
Tosca Digital, page 17
Musyarofahbttohirnur, page 19
Ahmad Safarudin, pages 21, 25, 31, 37, 39, 54, 58
Mikhail Gnatuyk, page 23
Rahimovarufana, page 33
Derplan Xiii, page 35
Victoria Rusyn, page 43
Anker, page 45
Margolana, page 47
Danoeng, page 50
Navalnyi, page 52
Oleksandr Khoma, page 56

Also from Lote Tree Press

A Kaleidoscope of Stories:
Muslim Voices in Contemporary Poetry

Symphonies of Theophanies:
Moroccan Meditations
by Peter Dziedzic

All the Birds were Invited to a Feast in the Sky
by Soukeyna Osei-Bonsu

From this Street to the Moon
by Nabila Jameel

The Well at the Desert's Heart:
Verses of Healing
by Tony Bowland

Light Steps:
A Poem on the Seerah of Prophet Muhammad ﷺ
by Ali Scully

Peace Be Upon Us

by Iljas Baker

Pauses on the Path

by Idris Mears

Milton Keynes UK
Ingram Content Group UK Ltd.
UKHW022221180823
427015UK00012B/81